Tot

Not my will, but Thy will be done.

Stacey Loper

Joshua 1:9

"Have I not commanded you? Be strong and courageous. Do not be frightened, and do not be dismayed, for the Lord your God is with you wherever you go."

Total Surrender

Copyright © 2017 by Stacey Loper

Request for information should be sent to:
info@staceyloper.com

ISBN 978-0-578-19505-6

Edited by: Jamie Wright and Tarika Coleman
Cover Design by: Stacey Loper and Roderickus Pickens @ Megamix Graphics

All rights reserved. No part of this book may be reproduced or transmitted in any form or by any means without written permission from the author.

Scriptures quoted are from the ESV (English Standard Version, 2007) or the NASB (National American Standard Bible, 1995).

Printed in USA

Dedication

To Tee Tee,
Thank you for embracing me before, during and after my transformation. Since I can remember, you have always been intentional about being active in our lives, when you didn't have to. I love you dearly!

To daddy, (Reginald Williams)
Thank you for giving me a voice. As a young woman, you showed me how to have a voice among my peers and elders. You told me not everyone would receive my truth well, but to always stay true to myself and whose I am. Thank you for the teachable moments that I believe, you weren't even aware of. I appreciate and love you more than you'll EVER know.

To my mother,
Thank you for showing me how to appreciate the noise. In my appreciation for the noise, I learned how to enjoy the calm. I love you mom!

To my father (Rudy Bailey),
Thank you for being my pillow. When I needed a soft spot, you provided the right amount of comfort. I loved you first!

TABLE OF CONTENTS

Foreward	7
Preface	9
The Yielding	17
YOU HAVE LOST YOUR MIND! SURRENDER YOUR THOUGHTS	23
WHAT LENS ARE YOU USING? SURRENDER YOUR CIRCUMSTANCES	33
THE KITCHEN (A FRUIT OF THE SPIRIT EXPERIENCE) SURRENDER YOUR LIFESTYLE	43
THE COEXISTENCE SURRENDER YOUR HEALING	53
WHY DID YOU STAY? SURRENDER YOUR MARRIAGE	65
I'M AT MY WHITS END! SURRENDER YOUR CHILDREN	73

THIS IS NOT WHERE I'M SUPPOSE TO BE   83
SURRENDER YOUR CAREER

OH, THAT'S BENEATH ME   97
SURRENDER YOUR LEADERSHIP

THE ENVELOP   105
SURRENDER YOUR FINANCES

NOT THE ONE   117
SURRENDER YOUR PERSONAL RELATIONSHIPS

ACKNOWLEDGEMENTS   125

Foreword

Jeremiah 29:11 For I know the plans I have for you," declares the LORD, "plans to prosper you and not to harm you, plans to give you hope and a future.

Born in Meridian, MS in a small tightknit community, Stacey has always had big dreams. With many odds stacked against her, through many challenges, mistakes and miscues - God was strategically orchestrating His plans for her life every step of the way. The move to New York to live with her father during her teenage years, played a pivotal role which allowed her dreams and aspirations to grow even larger.

When I first met Stacey in February 2005, she was working at the University of Southern Mississippi. I found Stacey to be a very beautiful, attractive and sexy young lady.

Now there was also the flipped side of unwelcoming characteristics - she was arrogant, insecure, selfish, bossy and needy; which some things have yet to change (she's still bossy and needy), but I'm her husband, I can say that about her.

Throughout a lifetime, we rarely come across a person who impacts your life beyond your wildest dreams. And dare I suggest it is just as rare to watch someone's life transform right before your eyes. A transformation so amazing, if not witnessed in person, it would be hard to believe.

Well, to the reader about to take this awesome journey leading us to total surrender.......Get READY to be wowed and blessed as you read this very transparent, informative, inspirational and spirit filled book. I could not be more proud of my wife, Stacey Loper, for walking out her purpose in God and giving me the opportunity to be her biggest and most influential supporter.

I pray this book impacts your life as well as many others you know and equips you in beginning the journey to a life of "Total Surrender".

Joaquin Loper,
Man of God, Husband and Father

PREFACE

I was having a conversation with an old friend who seemed confused about what he calls the drastic change I'd made in my life. As I continued to listen to him describe the girl he knew 20, 15, even 10 years ago and then began to compare her to the woman he was having the current conversation with, I smiled. The words "you've changed," had an impact on my heart and I knew I was doing something right.

"How do you know God is the reason for your change, that He even exist," he boldly asked.

In response to his question, I asked him, "How do you know the wind blows?" He responds with a chuckle.

I boldly continued to explain, "You know the wind blows because you can feel it. You feel it upon your face on a brisk, cold morning as you're walking to your car. You see the wind blowing by watching the leaves crawl across the ground as you're taking a bike ride. The same reasons you believe the wind blows but can't see it, are the same reasons I believe in God and that He is a significant part of the reason my life has changed."

Just like you can feel the wind blow, I can feel God in my heart. I can see what He is doing in my life by reflecting back over my life and realizing I don't look like what I've been through.

My response was not an attempt to make him believe in what I do (an omnipresent God, who sits high and looks low; can perform miracles, was born from a virgin, died and rose on the third day; forgives and loves unconditionally), but it was merely a response to make him realize, no matter who he thought he was describing (a manipulative, selfish, proud, arrogant, and exciting girl), I know who I am and whose I am.

My change occurred when I made the decision to surrender; the decision to put aside my childish ways and become a new creature in Christ. For a large portion of my life, I didn't know who I was. I was chasing this world, saying my name and didn't even know who I was talking about. I was getting tired, out of breath, but I wanted every breath to count. But how? How would I know what mattered? What words would I say that meant something to someone? Or even to me for that matter. What was to be my first step?

I was at church one Sunday and my Pastor said 'there's deliverance in your tears.' I was crying profusely and didn't know why. After he said that, I made my way to the alter, fell to my knees and began to let the shackles fall off my feet and I finally released the weights of all my fears, disappointments, doubts, and shame I'd been piling on my shoulders for years. That was the moment I decided I would not go back to that life of deceit and guilt. I wanted to be free, and that Sunday, I surrendered.

To surrender means *to cease resistance to an enemy or opponent and submit to authority.*

Did you catch that? *To cease resistance to an 'enemy' or 'opponent' and submit to authority.*

Before you surrender, you first have to identify that there's an enemy or an opponent involved.

See that's the problem. When you're struggling in your marriage, your finances, your children are acting up sideways, you feel lonely, or you can't seem to shake that sickness that has rendered you weak, you don't see it as an opponent that has a higher authority to answer to.

That's your first mistake.

Secondly, you have to decide how much of this beat down you're going to take before you just throw in the towel and surrender it to the One who can give you a loving and fulfilling marriage, prosperity in your finances, obedient children, comfort in your singleness and healing in your body.

*****

It's not enough for you to go day in and day out, feeling you have all the answers to your problems. You go to a job every day to earn an honest living for your family, yet, you're still living pay check to pay check, borrowing from Peter to pay Paul and still there is no way of seeing how you can save and plan for the future.

*****

You're doing all the right things in your marriage, so you think, but your spouse shows no vested interest in the marriage. Your spouse doesn't want to have conversation after a long workday has ended. Social media takes up most of their time and those extracurricular activities have multiplied in the past year. You haphazardly receive an 'I Love You' and a kiss before they leave in the morning, but it means nothing to you. You're tired. You feel like you're in this marriage alone. Your coworker begins to get a little comfortable, telling you how nice you look and how your new hair cut really highlights the contours of your eyes. You haven't heard in a long time how beautiful you are and your spouse has not recognized, in two weeks, that you've cut your hair. Married but feeling lonely. What do you do?

*****

It's a week before Good Friday and the Easter weekend. You're home visiting the in-laws for a family member's birthday party. Due to last minute plans, you decide that you, the husband and the kids would spend the night at your mother's house.

It's 1:00 A.M. in the morning and your little brother runs into the room where you're sleeping, yelling, "Where's my mama? They shot my brother. They shot my brother."

Waking in a panic, not really knowing what's going on, you jump from the bed asking your brother to calm down and talk to you. He continues screaming, "They shot my brother. Go get my mama." Then he rushes out the door. Left standing in the middle of my mother's kitchen eight months pregnant; what do you do when you're left with the last words of your little brother, "They shot my brother."

Do you recognize the opponent in the above scenarios?

Every day you allow yourself to suffer through situations such as these, you find yourself deeper than you were the day before and barely able to keep your head above water.

In your surrender, there's freedom from bondage. In your surrender, there's a peace that surpasses all understanding. In your surrender, there's a joy that no one can take from you, because you learn, the joy of the Lord is your strength.

16

THE YIELDING

You are reading these pages because I was obedient to what God was giving me at certain times in my life. I made a conscious decision to yield my will to the will of God and allow Him to operate through me for His glory.

There were times I wanted to sleep, but God was giving me the words he needed me to write in this book for you. There were times I wanted to be at a movie with my husband, but God sat me down to hear a relevant word from Him so I could go tell the next person that God is waiting on them to trust Him. There were many nights I wanted to sit down in my living room, on my comfortable sofa, with my delicious cup of coffee and watch re-runs of Chicago Fire, season two, but God needed me praying for my sisters and brothers in Christ so they could get a breakthrough in their marriages, their finances, to help get a grip on their children and to help them get back their passion to serve Him.

In my transformation, I had to surrender to being obedient. There was a yielding that had to take place in my heart and in my will. There were many things I wanted to be doing other than writing this book or opening up a business; but God had this blueprint laid out for me and I had some decisions to make.

I had to start believing that I could sleep after I've completed my assignment. I could go see a movie another day and my sofa wasn't going anywhere. I could get back to those things that satisfied my flesh later, but first, I had an assignment to fulfill and God was giving me clear instructions on how to maneuver through the task He'd given me and I couldn't be distracted.

It is God's timing, not yours. Always remember that. I'm awake writing at 2:00 AM because God has something He needs me to share with His people. This is not by choice, but on purpose.

You missed it.

God has a plan and a purpose for our lives. We miss the boat when we continuously tell ourselves we can get back to Gods work later and continue with our worldly life until it no longer satisfies us. God intentionally stops us in our tracks because He has something more meaningful, more impactful for us to do.

Are you willing to yield to God's calling?

Someone is waiting for you to encourage them, but because you are too busy fulfilling what's scheduled on your daily calendar, you are missing the opportunity to bless someone who just lost their job, lost a family member, has low self-esteem, marriage is suffering, children are being disobedient.

This book is meant to encourage you. To encourage you to take up your cross and follow Him; to give up the fight and surrender to God, those things that have made you lose your hope, your peace and your joy.

When you surrender, you will find freedom that you never thought you were deserving of. When you surrender, you will find that it is much easier to be a blessing to someone else rather than focusing on how someone else can be a blessing to you. When you surrender, you will see the glory of the Lord shine through you and give others hope that there is a way to live life abundantly here on earth.

It is my desire that as you read these pages, you will allow God to purposely take over the battles you are facing. Don't be afraid to take your hands and plans off your situation and let God do what He is going to do in it.

It starts right now.

Are you ready?

To surrender.

Scriptures that helped me in my surrender:

Cast all your cares on Him; for He cares for you.
1 Peter 5:7

"My Father, if you are willing, let this cup of suffering be taken from me. Yet, I want Your will to be done, not mine.
Luke 22:4

"For what does it profit a man to gain the whole world, but loses his own soul?"
Mark 8:36

YOU HAVE LOST YOUR MIND!

SURRENDER YOUR THOUGHTS

What do you believe is the truth about yourself? When you wake up in the morning, take a good look at yourself in the mirror, what do you see? Do you believe what the enemy is telling you about yourself? You're ugly, you aren't worthy, you're a bad person, you won't have any success in your life because of your past, and the many other negative images he's giving you as you stand there looking at your reflection in the mirror. Is that who you see? Or do you believe what God says you are? You are victorious, a conqueror, a man/woman of God, an overcomer, righteous, beautiful, worth dying for, transformed, forgiven and I can go on and on, but you get my point.

Every day you wake up, you have a choice. A choice to choose life or death, good or evil, victory or defeat. The Bible tells us to submit ourselves to God. Resist the devil and he WILL flee (James 4:7). The problem is you're not resisting the devil because many of you are looking at yourselves in the mirror and believing the images that he is assigning to you. You are giving him an opportunity to have authority in your life and hold your thoughts captive.

Surrender!

It's time for a TKO! It's your training day saints. Today is the day you stand in front of that mirror, against your opponent and go to battle. Tell your opponent, 'he is a liar!' You are more than what he says you are. Start speaking God's word over your life. Look yourself right in the eyes and tell yourself, 'I am fearfully and WONDERFULLY made (Psalms139:14). No matter the mistakes I've made, I'm already forgiven. I forgive myself (Acts 3:19). I am loved (Romans 5:8). The joy of the Lord is my strength (Nehemiah 8:10). I am more than a conqueror (Romans 8:37). I am not the sum of my past mistakes. I am whole in Christ Jesus. I am the head and not the tail. I am above and not beneath. I am a lender and not a borrower (Deuteronomy 28:12-13).

Declare God's word over your life daily; especially in those moments when the enemy is trying to make you believe you are less than what God has said you are. That's how you resist the devil and show him that you have surrendered his scheme to an authority who has more power than him.

Having total control over your thoughts is a daily exercise. It's something you must practice daily and choose to believe God's word upon and into your life. The Bible clearly instructs us to "speak those things that aren't as though they were" (Romans 4:17.) You may not have evolved into that multi-million-dollar entrepreneur you want to be; don't stop speaking that over your life. You may not have the peace you are seeking in your life right now because you are still making some needed changes to get past the struggles you have; don't stop asking God for that peace in your situation. Just because it doesn't look like the sun is going to shine on you today doesn't mean that God isn't working behind the scenes to give you what you are asking for. My Pastor always says, "The teacher is quiet when the student is testing." God doesn't say anything when He is testing you. He's waiting to give you your final grade so you can use it as a testimony to get others into the Kingdom.

There's a war going on and it's against the flesh and the spirit for the right to claim the minds of God's people. We receive reassurance in II Corinthians chapter 10, that if our weapons are mighty in God, we can pull down strongholds, cast down any argument and every high thing that goes against the knowledge of God. In this, we are able to bring every thought into captivity to the obedience of Christ.

My husband and I began to walk out the above scripture in our life in February 2017. We'd recently come off twenty-one days of fasting and praying with our church. Prior to starting the fast, we sat down as a family and began to write down everything we were asking God for in our marriage, for our children, in our finances, for wisdom in our day to day walk with Him, for favor in this season of our life, not just favor with God, but favor with man also. By the time we'd completed our list of specifics, we had two pages of things we were asking God to make clear to us during those twenty-one days.

Well needless to say, I'm completing this book in 2017 because God bought the vision into focus for me that writing books would be one of the creative financial increases for my family. However, there was another specific assignment God was bringing into focus for us that I couldn't seem to align my thoughts to agree with.

My thoughts were under attack. During the fasting and praying, I kept getting some really bad headaches. My stomach wasn't always in agreement with my body when I'd eat and I really can't explain it, but to say that I felt pressure building up in me like a soda being shaken and the pressure wasn't being released.

Within the twenty-one days of fasting and praying, we also did three days of absolute fasting and continuous praying. The first confirmation came when I picked up my Bible to read on the first night of the absolute fasting day and I turned to Joshua chapter 1 and pointed directly to verse 9. I nodded my head in agreement and said, "Yes God."

The second confirmation came immediately after the twenty-one days of fasting and praying when I began to read the online devotional, 'Through the Bible in One Year.'

Every day before starting the devotional, I was instructed to pray and ask God for what I was hoping to get from his word on that day. After asking, the next steps were to read the scriptures or books of the Bible outlined in the devotional, reflect on the verses/books and then respond to them in prayer. The first day I started the devotional was February 15th, 2017 and here is my ask, read, reflect, and respond as written in my journal that morning @ 7:45am

Ask: Speak to my heart Lord. Give me clear and concise directions and I will follow. Amen

Read: Luke 5:27-39, Genesis 1 and 2, and Psalms 1

Reflect: God is telling me to follow Him. The passage is a clear reminder that God is guiding me on this faith journey I'm on. There are some things He's cleaning up in me for me

to be in right standing with Him and with Man. Like God created the Heaven and the earth with specific instructions, He is instructing me to create something that is currently formless as the earth was before His creation. Create it in His likeness and it will be blessed. Do not be unrighteous in any way or do business with anyone who is untrustworthy. Meditate on His word daily. Continue to be guided by God and you will prosper.

Respond: God I'm yours. I will be that light. I will submit to your will and your way in my life. Strengthen me to withstand the opposition. Daily, I put on the full armor of God as I prepare to do the work of the Lord. I will follow you and leave EVERYTHING behind. In Jesus name, Amen.

This wasn't a coincidence. This was a divine intervention that God had set up specifically for me. I didn't know the first scripture would be Jesus saying "Follow Me."

Every scripture after that set forth the blueprint for the events that happened next.

About a week after reading day one of the devotional, I was driving to work and God spoke a word to me with the name of the business my husband and I were to open. For a minute, I looked dumbfounded and I heard it again. I immediately picked up the phone, called my husband and shared with him what I'd just been given. He was amazed at the named and thought it was well suited for what we were about to do.

After the name, came the completed blueprints for our new business **Beyond Words**. It was so overwhelming. The download was coming and it wasn't stopping. We knew exactly where we would be located, what our tag line would be, what our website was going to look like, what the business plan entailed, what services we'd offer, an opening date, and a marketing strategy. Within days, everything was on paper and ready to be executed.

I had to yield to God's words over my life and what He already had in store for me. I couldn't see it because I was blinded by the mortgage that was due on the first of the month; the truck note that was due by the fifteenth and the light bill that had to be paid if I wanted to keep the lights on for my family.

    I was my own hindrance. I wouldn't allow my thoughts to align with what God said because I couldn't see how, financially, we were going to make it happen with just one income at that time. Let me be honest, I was walking by sight and not by faith; oh but God! Jeremiah 29:11, there is no way I could've ever imagined this is what God had waiting for me. It was a total surrender that allowed me to bring every thought into captivity of the obedience of Christ.

Scriptures that helped me in my surrender:

Have I not commanded you! Be strong and courageous. Do not be afraid, do not be discouraged, for the Lord your God will be with you wherever you go.
Joshua 1:9

Seek ye first His Kingdom and His righteousness, and all these things will be added unto you.
Matthew 6:33

For though we walk in the flesh, we do not war according to the flesh. For the weapons of our warfare are not carnal, but mighty in God for pulling down strongholds, casting down arguments and every high thing that exalts against the knowledge of God, bringing every thought into captivity to the obedience of Christ.
2 Corinthians 10:3-5

WHAT LENS ARE YOU USING?

SURRENDER YOUR CIRCUMSTANCES

You're sitting at home crying your eyes out. You wish you didn't have to live this life. You'd rather be dead; maybe then people wouldn't have to deal with you just because you're their coworker, their parent, daughter, son, sister, brother or cousin. You're consumed by the loneliness.

"What is so wrong with me?" you keep asking yourself.

You take a look at yourself in the mirror that morning and you scream to the top of your lungs, "I HATE MY LIFE!"

*****

Your choices in life are a direct result of your current circumstances. You became a mother at sixteen. Your life was snatched away after a one night stand with your high school crush. You're lost. A teenage mother, clueless with nowhere to turn, you did the best you could do. Starting at the age of eight, your son was being molested by his uncle, your brother, over and over and over again, for five years. So caught up in living your own life, you turned a blind eye to the sign that presented itself when you found blood stains in his underwear. You asked him was everything okay; of course he said things were fine. At age eleven, he became very rebellious against you and began running away from home. Back and forth you go with him, 3 years pass and you find out about the manipulation, molestation and the secrets your family held from you. You're his mother, you were supposed to protect him. Guilt, shame, defeat and low self-worth begin to take root in your heart.

You've paid for ten years of counseling and have apologized a thousand times, hoping your money and an apology would help him forgive you. He's 25 years old, struggling with his sexuality and you're the last person he wants to turn to for help.

*****

Your father was never there for you. He never showed up to any of your high school football games for four years. You watched him physically and emotionally abuse your mother while having an extramarital relationship with the woman down the street. You have tried convincing yourself that it's okay; your grown now and there are no hard feelings there. You're 32 years old with two sons, a daughter and a beautiful wife and now your father would like to come visit and meet the family. You're angry at him and so full of bitterness and un-forgiveness that you just stare at his number scrolling across the screen of your phone; and when you do answer, you give him the excuse, "timing just isn't right." You're praying and asking God, 'why is your heart so hardened toward this man.' You've said over and over again you've forgiven him, but when you are faced with the reality of having to interact with him, you just can't seem to get pass the tightness in your chest and the lump in your throat.

*****

You have no peace, you are desperate for some hope that life gets better, but you are so tired of waiting. You don't know the first step to getting out of the pit you're in and you wouldn't even know who to ask for help at this point. No one wants to be bothered with you anyway. Your bitterness has made you blind to the love of the people around you. You have not recognized the sincere love of those who were placed in your life to help you get past the pain of a broken home, verbal abuse from your mother and an unwanted abortion. You have been scarred for life; so you think. After your parents made you have an abortion at the age of 16 because they didn't want to be shamed by the pregnancy of their teenage daughter, you've built a wall to prevent others from letting you down and hurting you more than you've already been hurt by the people who were supposed to love you unconditionally. Your motto is trust no one; You've been doing this thing called life all alone, why change it now.

Say this out loud; "My God is bigger than my circumstances." Scream, "My God is bigger than my circumstances!"

Do you really believe that? You couldn't if you're sitting at the bottom of your pit and the slime of your self-pity is making it impossible for you to climb out. All things are possible with God (Matthew 19:26). Now come out the pit. You can do it! Come out; now surrender.

If I tell you this will be easy, I will be lying to you. However, I can tell you this, your pity can be your potential. Your pity can be the very thing that will make you want to get up and walk again. It can be the one thing that will cause you to step out on faith and trust yourself to love without resisting what God has for you. You have the ability to take authority over your life and choose to turn things around for your own good.

I've been there, done that, and bought the t-shirt for it. I thought I would never have the strength to turn from my wicked ways. I'd been doing dirty, nasty, shameful things for so long, that I wasn't sure if I even had any good left in me. It didn't happen overnight, but as time progressed, I began to read more, pray more, meditate on God's word, declare His promises over my life, tithe, serve and love God's people right where they were, and I started seeing my circumstances differently. Instead of looking through an unfocused lens at all the negative, berating, unnecessary things, I began to focus in on what God had waiting for me in the distance. Instead of concentrating on those things that never came into focus, no matter how long I manipulated my lens, I had to change my target and seek God's plan and purpose for my life.

During my infancy walk with Christ, I began to take a look back over the past fourteen years of my life. As I watched what was going on around me and the people I was impacting, I was ashamed. I was disgusted. I began to see all the hurt I was inflicting on the ones I proclaimed to love, was the hurt I had not resolved within myself. I couldn't blame anyone for the hell I was going through but me. My circumstances were a direct result of the choices I'd made and like I said before, the end result wasn't worth bragging about.

It was a sincere cry out for help that caused my paradigm shift. At that moment, I became vulnerable. I made the choice to allow all my pain to be exposed in front of those who were watching. I was prepared to become naked and unashamed of the person I was. I was ready to be made new. What about you? Are you ready for a paradigm shift?

SURRENDER! Release the situations that have kept you in bondage.

The mother of the young man in the scenario at the beginning of this chapter has seen first-hand what surrendering can do in an individual's life. It wasn't easy for her to trust what God was doing in that situation, but her paradigm shift came when she agreed to fast and pray with me two years ago. Her fasting and praying was for forgiveness toward her brother and the bitterness and anger she carried for him and herself.

Depressed for many years, stricken with grief, guilt, and shame of what her brother had done, her lack of parenting, and what her son had become as a result of it, she was at the end of her ropes. She couldn't see the forest for the trees and everything around her was grey. But God! We prayed together several times a day, dispatching Angels, placing God's words on her request, asking God to change her heart, binding those spirits that consumed her and her brother. She began walking in forgiveness and for the first time in years, she was able to look at her brother, tell him she loved him and hug him without the bitterness she'd once felt at the mention of his name. She didn't forgive him for his sake, but for her own. After the fast, she called me early one Sunday morning and said, "I finally understand that we fight not against flesh and blood (Ephesians 6:12), I had no reason to be mad at him when it was the enemy the entire time. That curse was generational. It was handed down to him from our bloodline. He just didn't know how to fight it."

She acknowledged her opponent and she surrendered him to the appropriate authority, Jesus. The enemy no longer has power over her; she served him an eviction notice. As for her son, through prayer and supplication, their relationship is shifting. She is trusting God to show her how to guide him while on this walk and she is being still and allowing God to give her the words to say and the actions to take that will show him Gods love in people and in this world. She understands there is a time for everything under the sun. She's letting God show her His promises.

The scenarios in this chapter may not be yours, but you have an opponent and in order to address the need in your life, you first have to notice what the need is. Before you can take authority over your opponent, you first have to recognize the opponent. Whether your opponent is addiction, lust, pornography, adultery, fear, deceit, sexuality, fornication, loneliness, pride; whatever it is, surrender it to its' rightful authority and watch your life take on new meaning.

Your current circumstances aren't the end for you. You don't have to take a seat where you are. There's more for you, you just have to keep going in the midst of all the noise, the chaos, the turmoil. Find your strength in His joy. It will be amazing. You will be in awe!

Scriptures that helped me in my surrender:

For our struggle is not against flesh and blood, but against the rulers, against the powers, against the world forces of this darkness, against the spiritual forces of wickedness in heavenly places. Ephesians 6:12

Rejoice in hope, be patient in tribulation, be constant in prayer. Romans 12:12

And let us not grow weary in well doing, for in due season we will reap, if we do not give up.
Galatian 6:9

THE KITCHEN

A FRUIT OF THE SPIRIT EXPERIENCE
SURRENDER YOUR LIFESTYLE

What do you do when you're left standing in the middle of your mother's kitchen, eight months pregnant, hearing the last words of your little brother, 'They shot my brother.' before he rushes out the door to the scene of a crime, where your oldest brother lay dead.

For me and my family, our world completely shifted at 1:00 A.M. that night.

When we went to bed, never, in a million years, did we think we'd awake under the above circumstances; but that's the beauty in this aspect of my surrender.

It was a week before Good Friday. My husband's aunt was turning forty-five and her children were having her a surprise birthday party. Initially, me, my husband, and my mother-in-law weren't going to attend the party due to our work schedules and the fact that I was eight months pregnant and fifty-two pounds heavier than normal. However, we decided, at the last minute, that we'd make it a quick trip down to Meridian and come right back to Memphis early the next morning.

Due to it being last minute, I called my mother to see if we could stay at her house for the night since we didn't make other sleeping arrangements prior to the weekend. Of course, she obliged. However, she had to work overnight that evening and left the key in our usual place for us to enter into the house.

It's 1:00 A.M., my little brother comes running into the room where my husband and I are sleeping, yelling, 'Where's my mama? They shot my brother, they shot my brother.'

Awaking to those words completely startled me. I rose from the bed trying to get my brother to calm down and talk to me. My husband and I follow him into the kitchen where he continues screaming, 'Go get my mama. They shot my brother.' Then he storms out the house.

Left standing in the middle of my mother's kitchen, I'm staring my husband in the eyes, trying to process my brother's words.

I managed to snap out of the dazed state and my mind begin processing the information I was given.

In one breathe, I ran to the back room, picked up my cell phone, and said to my husband, "Get the keys, we have to get my mama from work."

In the three-minute ride it took us to get to my mother's job, we'd discussed how we would strategically get her to come home with us without giving her too much information. We knew we had to get her to the house before we could tell her the reason she had to immediately leave work.

First, I spoke with her manager about having to get her from work due to a family emergency. Without giving the manager too much information, she was very understanding and took me to the area my mother was working in. Surprised to see me, the first thing she asked me was, 'Stacey, what's going on? Why are you here? Is everything okay?'

I responded very calmly, "you need to come with me. Something has happened to Donyale."

She began to panic and ask a lot of questions. I couldn't answer her because I didn't have a lot of details. The three-minute drive back to the house seemed more like thirty. When we pulled into the driveway, my aunt and her children had just pulled up to the house.

Now my mother is asking more questions. I shared with her that Donyale had been shot at his home in Jackson, MS and the ambulance is just arriving.

As I was explaining it to her, she was screaming about having to leave to go to Jackson right that moment and asking what hospital they're taking him to. While I'm trying to keep her calm and explain things to her, my phone began to ring and the call was coming from my oldest brother's, (who'd just been shot) phone.

I walked away from my mother to answer the call, knowing that there may not be good news on the other end of the receiver.

As soon as I answered the call, I stated, "Just tell me what hospital they're taking him to and we're on the way."

The last words I wanted to hear rang in my ear like an alarming smoke detector; "They pronounced him dead on the scene."

I'd like to say time stopped, although I know it didn't, but all I could do was press the end call button and glance over at my mom from afar.

I immediately called my step father to let him know what was going on and to get his input into how I should handle telling my mother my brother was dead. My dad shared with me how important it was that I tell her the news. He made it clear that allowing her to get on the road before knowing what she would be faced with would be unfair and detrimental to her. I reassured him I'd do it before letting her go to Jackson and I'd call him back in a little while.

I walked back over to my mother. As everyone was asking questions, they all sounded muffled and as though they were speaking to me from a distance. All I was laser beam focused on was my mother's face as I approached her.

I asked her to go into the house and have a seat for a minute. I needed her to settle herself before I gave her the news. She was very hesitant, but I managed to get her to go in the house for a minute and just sit down. I believe telling my mother that her son was dead was the hardest thing I've ever had to tell her.

Where does the beauty in our brokenness come from in this situation?

I've learned that God will position you right where he needs you to be so that others may see His glory through you.

In the exact moments on March 31st, 2012, there was no way I could've told you that the peace of God surrounded me or that I surrendered to it; but that is exactly what happened.

It wasn't until after the funeral that my cousin explained to me the extraordinary peace she saw operating in me that night. I didn't display many emotions, she explained. From her depiction of events, she tells that I was very rational, reassuring and compassionate.

See, it wasn't my plan to be at my mother's house that night. I was there on purpose; on assignment.

I didn't realize it but God was equipping me months earlier for that very night. My life hadn't always been about trusting God, allowing His will to be done, or saturated with prayer. Never did I imagine I'd have to play such an intricate role in creating an atmosphere of comfort and peace for my family.

What I finally realized, after all the noise subsided and people went back to their day to day activities is this; God was testing me to see if I would trust him to give me a peace that surpassed all understanding. To be honest with you, had it not been for the yielding, the surrender that I'd committed to months prior, I believe my testimony would have a different ending.

March 31st, 2012 is an event that transformed our family dynamics. It's one of the events in my life that gave me a huge appreciation for God's grace and His mercy. Without His mercy, there wouldn't have been peace for my family. Without His grace, the unity we experienced as a family wouldn't have been created. Without total surrender, my fruit wouldn't have been present for others to experience.

Scriptures that helped me in my surrender:

Submit yourself to God completely. Reach out your hands to Him for help.
Job 11:13

Don't let anyone look down on you because you are young, but set an example for the believers in speech, in conduct, in love, in faith and in purity.
1 Timothy 4:12

"I am the vine, you are the branches. He who abides in Me, and I in him, bears much fruit; for without Me you can do nothing."
John 15:5

THE COEXISTENCE

SURRENDER YOUR HEALING

You believe in the healing power of Jesus Christ. You see it performed time after time at church and you hear about it from friends, family, and neighbors. The healing power of Jesus Christ is real and when you see His power manifest itself upon your peers, you rejoice and praise Him.

★ ★ ★ ★ ★

Now it's your turn. You just received a medical diagnosis that has given you a death sentence of six months or less.

★ ★ ★ ★ ★

Your outcome from the long term disability evaluation has rendered you weak and dependent upon the people around you for support and mental stability.

★ ★ ★ ★ ★

Your Obstetrician just shared words of sorrow with you because there's nothing he can do to save your baby. Your body is going to spontaneously abort your pregnancy. This isn't the first or the second time your body has disappointed you, but the third.

Believing in healing is easy when you aren't the one seeking to be healed. When you've been diagnosed with an illness in your body, intruders (the enemy) begin to come in and make you forget the plan and purpose God has for your life. Because the flesh and the spirit coexist, affliction of the body will make you forget whose you are.

A quick reminder; you are a child of God, therefore, you are led by the spirit, not by the flesh. As a child of God, His word should always ring pleasurable when you have been faced with a medical diagnosis or life changing experience. However, what usually happens in situations as this is you quickly turn your focus to the problem and not the problem solver. You talk about the problem so much that you make it seem bigger than your faith and the God you serve. That medical diagnosis knocked you off your feet. Unexpected and abrupt as it was, the only thing that kept ringing in your head was the confirmation that you were severely ill; that your baby wasn't going to make it. Too soon you submitted to the affliction of your flesh and expected your spirit to conform to the flesh instead of using the authority you have to command your flesh to conform to your spirit.

You've got power! Activate it, apply it, and watch what God will do when you trust, believe and have faith in His word and His wonder working power that also works through you. Yes, your body aborted the baby you so desperately wanted and now you're giving up all hope of being a mother. What God has for you is for you; in His timing. That successful pregnancy may come two years later, blessing you with more than you could ask or think.

I remember having to be rushed to the emergency room in May 2015. It was late on a Tuesday evening. For days I'd felt like I was on fire from the inside out, but it was centrally located in one area on my back. It was a tingling, itching and very irritating pain that worsened and spread as days past. My muscles in my upper body were very sore as if I'd been working them for days at a time and I was extremely tired.

We arrived at the emergency room, I checked in, gave them my symptoms and waited to be called to a room by the nurse practitioner. After a forty-two-minute wait, she called me in, looked over my complaints listed on the intake form and asked me to point to the area where I was feeling the most pain. I showed her and she then asked me to describe the pain again because she didn't see any signs of irritation as I explained it on my intake form. I began to explain very vividly, I felt like my back and my breast were on fire. I explained to her how I just wanted to scratch myself through to the bone to possibly feel some relief. I also shared with her that the pain was spreading from the middle of my back to under my right arm to my right breast; I just felt like ripping my breast off at that point. I was tired, irritated and sore.

"You have shingles Mrs. Loper," she said.

"Shingles, you gotta be kidding me," I replied.

"No ma'am," she responded and went to get the doctor.

Once the doctor came into the room, he confirmed the diagnosis, and explained to me the series of events that would possibly happen. A rash would form in the area I was currently experiencing the pain. The pain would worsen and as the rash formed, it would be sensitive to touch and very contagious. He even warned me that I may experience headaches, nausea, high fever and the symptoms could last for about ninety days.

"The devil is a lie," I said. "Shingles? How in the world did I get shingles?"

I was stunned. I really didn't understand it. I thought shingles were for old people. Ninety days of those symptoms? Absolutely not.

I recall not going to bible study the following evening. The pain was getting worse and within the past sixteen hours, the rash had surfaced. I was in a funk. I couldn't wear a shirt, so a tank top had to do. I was so fatigued and just wanted to sleep.

My husband returned home from bible study, recognized my poor state of mind and began praying for me. I was lying on an air mattress in the middle of my living room and he was walking through the house praying. I got up and grabbed the book, 'Prayer's That Rout Demons,' by John Eckhardt and began declaring God's word over my sickness. Needless to say, after praying and petitioning to God for nine straight days, the rash dried up and all symptoms and signs of the diagnosis vanished.

Now what if I hadn't aligned my spirit to lead my flesh into healing? What if I'd just allowed my flesh to remain weak and the sickness run its' course? The enemy would've tried to run that scheme on me every time he wanted me to doubt God; to get me outside God's will.

Executing the authority that was given to me by the God I serve issued the enemy his eviction notice; he had to leave at the sound of the name of Jesus. But what happens when you have a relationship with God, but you haven't tapped into the power that's inside you?

I had the pleasure of treating a beautiful and intelligent Cuban woman during my time in mental health. Very depressed, Isa came to receive what she felt was her last hope of ever having a quality of life; an alternative, non-drug treatment for major depressive disorder. During her consult, Isa shared that she was willing to do whatever it took to get emotionally and mentally stable enough to experience joy and what normal feels like.

The treatment consisted of five days a week treatments of stimulation to the prefrontal cortex of the brain for eight weeks total, that lasted about forty minutes in length each session. With the treatment, Isa received traditional talk therapy to help her resolve emotions that still carried weight in her life which was an added trigger to her depression. As Isa shared more and more about herself with me, she began to open old wounds and reveal emotions she'd repressed for many years. Migrating from Cuba at the age of sixteen, during Castro's reign, leaving everything she knew behind to start a new life with her mother and siblings, Isa felt like a fish out of water. Now there she was, in unfamiliar territory, the language barrier keeping her from being a part of the newness and understanding who she was as an individual; rejection, neglect, resentment and loneliness began to take root in her heart. Little did she know, those would be the very emotions holding her hostage and damaging every relationship she'd establish from the age of sixteen forward.

Forty years later and two divorces, tense relationship with her children, several medical diagnoses (including breast cancer), suicidal ideations, unstable relationships with the male species, and constant feelings of rejection, Isa just wanted to die if the only thing she had to look forward to every morning was waking up and looking depression in the face when she looked at herself in the mirror.

Depression was her enemy, and it was stealing, killing, and destroying the abundant life that she was promised to live. Isa was angry, and her anger was distracting her from hearing the voice of God.

Isa said to me one day, "If I could take off depression and put back on breast cancer, I would. It's measurable," she said, "I can have an x-ray, complete some blood work, have a mammogram; those things are able to tell me how severe my diagnosis is. Then there's support because people understand breast cancer and they can sympathize with me and my pain; but depression," she pauses, "it's slowly killing me Stacey, taking everything I love away because no one believes in it, it's untouchable, it's undetectable under a microscope and it's paralyzing," she shared as tears rolled down her face.

It was that day, Isa spoke those words, she handed her depression over to the authority.

Isa is being equipped with everything she needs to relinquish depression. Isa knows this won't be easy and it's not going to happen overnight, but she's committed to walking through that experience with her psychiatrist, her grief counselor and spiritual leaders. Isa is strengthening her spirit daily so she can correctly align her flesh to submit to her spirit. She's still putting those unresolved emotions to rest, one by one, but she is aware that she has to forgive first, not for the other person, but for herself. Isa is renewing her mind daily by meditating on God's word and speaking it over her life. She's on her way to total restoration and redemption because she knows the prayers of the righteous avail much and because she believes she's one of the righteous, God will heal her and give her back everything that was taken from her.

Scriptures that helped me in my surrender:

Fear not, for I am with you; be not dismayed, for I am your God; I will strengthen you, I will help you, I will uphold you with my righteous right hand.
Isaiah 41:10

Many are the afflictions of the righteous, but the Lord delivers him out of them all.
Psalms 34:19

"According to your faith, be it done to you."
Matthew 9:29

WHY DID YOU STAY?

SURRENDER YOUR MARRIAGE

"Why did you stay?" I asked my husband.

"Something wouldn't let me leave," he replied.

Six years ago, the above exchange was a brief part of a long conversation I had with my husband. It was his words that have stuck with me to this very day.

Marriage is a choice, no matter what you go through or the choices you/your spouse may make, to stick and stay.

Six years ago, I made some choices that gave my husband a valid and biblical reason to divorce me. As much as he was leaning toward taking our son and going on with his life without the pain and confusion I bought into our marriage, he stayed, because of a small still voice that told him to "Be Still".

As I've grown from an infant to a mature adult in Christ, I've come to realize what a major part Holy Spirit played in a situation that could've ended very badly; but God was working for my good when the enemy wanted me to believe everything was bad.

But it could've been different.

What if my husband would've chosen not to forgive me? What if he would've chosen to ignore that small still voice telling him to "Be Still?"

What if he would've chosen to react differently the night he found that text message in my inbox?

Our story could've been totally different from what it has turned out to be today. My husband chose to forgive me and start walking the path toward becoming emotionally and spiritually complete.

All odds were against me. I wasn't raised in a two parent household where my mother and father were married, shared their ups and downs, yet they still went to bed with one another every night, said I love you daily despite their differences, and showed me what love looked like. NOPE, that wasn't my life!

I never received the opportunity to see marriage done right as I grew up. My mindset was on living single and enjoying every minute of it no matter who I hurt in the process.

However, my husband had a different experience. He grew up with pictures of marriage right in front of him. From his grandparents being married 58 years, to his parent's marriage lasting 21 years before divorcing, and many of his aunts and uncles being married for many years as well. My husband was allotted the opportunity to see marriage and divorce from many perspectives. In those many different experiences, my husband knew that there were many choices he could make within his own marriage to strengthen it or to let it crumble.

He chose to strengthen it.

I remember hearing the fight in my husband's voice and seeing the pain in his eyes as we struggled through that dark place in our marriage. He never gave up.

Did he ever feel like giving up?

Absolutely! There were many days he shared with me how he just wanted to throw in the towel. For a long time, he wouldn't say, "I love you." And as much as my husband enjoys sex, there were times when the intimacy was very few and far between.

He needed time to heal and I needed to respect that. After all, I was the reason he was in so much pain. And through it all, he continued to respect me as his wife. I needed him to take as much time as it would take for him to be emotionally complete.

It could've been different!

I could've been the victim of a homicide that night.

My husband could've been serving a 15 year to life sentence for attempted murder/murder.

But he chose different.

He chose to try and understand what went wrong, if anything, and why. He chose to walk away from the situation that night because of what he felt like doing to me. He chose to seek God for guidance because he was about to lose his mind and his family.

The results?

An experience of complete forgiveness.

My husband and I both learned that although within the exchange was pain, there was also transformation. After the exchange, our spiritual walk catapulted to another level. We were determined to let the enemy know he had to leave. I opened the door and now I had to do everything within my power to get the enemy out and seal that door shut.

Together, my husband and I prayed continuously, received Godly counsel concerning what to do next to maintain our spiritual strength during the battle. It meant everything to us to show the enemy that we would NOT conform to this world, but we would be transformed by the renewing of our minds, and we had to be intentional about changing.

I don't know what my life would be like had my husband chose differently, and I really don't care. What I do know is this, I'm grateful that God saw fit to restore what was broken, redeem what was lost and forgive what had been dishonored. Because my husband trusted God, even when the odds were totally against us, we are walking in our purpose as a husband and a wife. His love for me covered my sins that had broken our marriage into pieces.

Our story may not be your story, but as we continue to walk in God's purpose for our lives, we hope that our story will encourage you to never give up, allow God to speak to your heart and listen to Him as He guides you through the brokenness, the darkness, the dry places and the doubt. "God is not a man that He shall lie"(Numbers 23:19), "His word will not return void"(Isaiah 55:11). He will end your brokenness and have you walking in purpose!

Be encouraged and although you may not be able to see what God is doing in your marriage or relationship, remember, "Faith is the substance of things hoped for and the evidence of things not seen"(Hebrews 11:1). There's beauty in your brokenness, our marriage is proof of that!

Scriptures that helped me in my surrender:

Therefore, what God has bought together,
let no one separate.
Mark 10:9

She brings him good, and not harm.
Proverbs 31:12

Above all, love each other deeply,
because love covers a multitude of sin.
1 Peter 4:8

I'M AT MY WHITS END.

SURRENDER YOUR CHILDREN

I received a phone call late one evening from a friend. She's a single mother with three kids, one daughter and two sons. Her daughter is fifteen, in her second year of high school and peer pressure is getting the best of her. Over the past three months, the daughter has been very rebellious. Talking back to her mother, coming in late from cheer practice, not keeping her mother informed of her location between practice and ball games. She insists on hanging with a group of girls that her mother believes is unhealthy for her, but the daughter just feels the mom doesn't want her to have a life as a teenager. Mom breaks down in tears as she continues to explain how she is completely drained from the battle she's been fighting with her daughter. "It's never ending; she challenges everything I say!" mom exclaims.

Mom works a full time job at a retail store that doesn't allow her the opportunity to be flexible for her children. Mom misses out on most of the ball games and extracurricular activities that her children are involved in due to her work schedule. She has a family support system but that only goes so far before they start wanting something in return. Mom feels guilty that she is unavailable for her daughter most of the time and is feeling that the rebellion is just a way to get a response from mom, but lately mom says she's been too exhausted to entertain the behavior and it's only getting worse. After a deep sigh, she asked, "What am I to do when I just can't keep fighting this battle?"

On one hand I was glad to hear that she recognized she was in a battle, but on the other, I was saddened that she had gone to battle with no armor. As she was sharing her experience with me, I began to pray. I was standing in the gap for her because she was clueless that her first weapon of defense should've been the word of God, however, she was being the best parent she knew how to be. She was becoming weary in her well doing and it was about to consume her.

I shared with her that my experience as a parent hasn't been a crystal stair. I reassured her that no matter how peachy my life may seem, it took times like what she's going through to get me and my family to peaceful destination. I shared with her that before my husband and I began reading the word on a consistent basis and equipping ourselves with the appropriate tools to help us parent God's way, we were completely lost in guiding our children on a path of purpose and understanding. We didn't know how to make discipline a learning opportunity. We had no clue about how to show our kids the right way by using God's word as a teaching tool for them to build with, making it relevant to what's going on within the environment they participate in daily. Like my friend, we were doing what we knew. We knew how to punish and when things got too out of hand we resorted to spanking. Until you know better.

Our oldest daughter was fourteen when we truly learned how to parent God's way.

Our daughter was fourteen when she wanted to start dating. She'd met this young boy at a local football game and after about a month of exchanging dialogue with him over the phone, she decided she liked him and wanted to call him her boyfriend. Well we weren't going for that. We shut that down rather quickly and hoped she'd just leave it alone.

Absolutely not!

Months go by and now she's fifteen and the school year is coming to an end. She decides to tell us again that she likes this boy and she would really like for us to give her a chance to just date him. Against everything my husband said, I asked him to give it a try. "Let's meet his parents," I said. "Let's see what his family is like." My husband was totally against it, especially since our daughter was fifteen and the boy was 18, but my husband decided to try it my way.

Wrong decision!

We caught pure hell from our daughter after meeting his parents. She wanted to go to his house all the time. She wanted to go to his prom with him and then came graduation. We did allow her to attend his graduation with him and his family, but that only made matters worse. After graduation, she felt we should allow her to see him whenever she wanted.

It was an early Summer afternoon. My husband was out working in a nearby neighborhood and I was home with our fifteen-year-old and two sons. Our fifteen-year-old comes into the kitchen to ask me if she could go to her friend's house to hang out with him. She explained that his mother was home so I had nothing to worry about. I said to her that I didn't think that was a good idea for today, maybe another day. All of a sudden, she begins ranting about how we NEVER let her do anything. We NEVER listen to how she feels. We NEVER give her the benefit of the doubt and on and on. I immediately turned to her and said, "If you don't like how we are raising you and you think someone else can do it better, you can leave, but you will leave with what you came with, NOTHING!"

She walked away, making smart remarks, went upstairs to put on a pair of sneakers and walked out our front door. Before I allowed myself to become angry with her, I picked up the phone, called my husband and told him if he didn't come get her, he wasn't going to have a daughter at the end of the day, if she continued to disrespect me.

My husband arrived home and found her on our neighbors' front porch waiting for them to let her in. He made her come back into the house so he could get a better understanding about the situation, but he couldn't get a word in edge wise because she was continuously ranting. By this time, emotions were flaring and things were escalating.

The last thing I was thinking about was what would Jesus do in this situation. I felt disrespected and embarrassed that my child would talk to me in such a manner. All I wanted to do was let her know who was the parent and who was the child. Words continued to fly from her mouth and I just couldn't take it anymore; I completely lost it. Before I knew it, I had one knee in her chest and both hands around her neck. I yelled at her saying, "You will not disrespect me or my husband in this house."

After realizing what I'd done, I released her from my grip, took a step back away from her and broke down crying. My entire body was shaking and I felt like I couldn't breathe. I was still an infant in my spiritual walk at that point in my life and to be quite honest, I began fighting that fight carnally and not spiritually. I was unequipped to fight that battle and the more the situation escalated, the more I realized how unprepared I was.

Needless to say, what the devil meant for bad, God turned it around for our good. The above situation we experienced with our daughter was pivotal to the relationship our family has with God today. That day taught us to be still and know that He is God. That day allowed not only us as parents to immediately recognize when the enemy is rearing its' ugly head, but it also allowed us the opportunity to use it as a teaching tool for our children to understand how relationships with their peer's effect more than just the moment they are living in. It was the day of the above incident that I surrendered my children to Christ.

It was hard. I felt I was losing all since of being a parent. I felt out of control, but I quickly learned it was because I was trying to hold on to the control, that my children were slowly slipping away from my grip.

God entrusted me with my children. It was a responsibility of mine to give them back to Him and allow Him to help me guide them into the plan and purpose He has for their lives.

Too often, as parents, you lose sight of what's best for your children because you're too busy looking at it from your own perspective. What's best for them may not be your best, but it's what God has for them. In order to get an understanding of that, you have to let go and let God. My decision to allow my fifteen-year-old to have conversation and spend time with an eighteen-year-old boy at that time was not God's best for her and I didn't listen. It didn't matter how unhappy that decision made her, it wasn't a wise decision on my behalf as a parent.

After sharing my story with my friend that night, I reassured her it gets better.

It's not going to happen overnight, but she needed to trust God in her situation. I encouraged her to stay on her knees and not cease in praying for her daughters' deliverance. I suggested to she not allow the pain of her daughters' disobedience to cause her to anger easily and respond or react harshly toward her daughter but to love her through the storm she's walking through. There were more issues there. No father in the home. A lot of resentment for her absent, neglectful father. Her daughter wanted to fit in and the environment she was placing herself in provided that comfort she needed to feel accepted. I shared with her that love covers a multitude of sin (1 Peter 4:8) and in loving her daughter comes comfort and understanding. Be firm and unmovable in how she disciplines her daughter and hold her accountable, I shared. It takes time, but through prayer and supplication, submit your request to God (Philippians 4:6) and He will give you the desires of your heart.

Scriptures that helped me in my surrender:

Love covers a multitude of sin
1 Peter 4:8

We fight not against flesh and blood, but against principalities, against powers, against the rulers of darkness of this world, against spiritual wickedness in high places.
Ephesians 6:12

Train up a child in the way he should go; even when he is old he will not turn from it.
Proverbs 22:6

Fathers, do not provoke your children to anger, but bring them up in the discipline and instruction of the Lord.
Ephesians 6:4

Folly is bound up in the heart of a child, but the rod of discipline drives it far from him.
Proverbs 22:15

THIS IS NOT WHERE I'M SUPPOSED TO BE

SURRENDER YOUR CAREER

"Good afternoon and thank you for being our guest. How many?"

How in the world did I get here?

A bachelor's degree in education with extensive training and experience in leadership and professional development, yet I'm a host at the local franchise restaurant? This is not where I'm supposed to be.

From Meridian, Mississippi, to New York City, to Dallas, Texas, to Hattiesburg, Mississippi, and to my final destination, Memphis, Tennessee. Fourteen years' experience in education, six of those in leadership and three in professional development training, and I'm a host at a restaurant. Do not despise small beginnings. God had me exactly where He needed me to be for that season in my life.

Once I arrived in Memphis, TN in 2006, I'd been in education for seven years. I was passionate about it and I just knew, teaching was my purpose. It's all I'd ever wanted to do, and to be honest, in my opinion, I was darn good at it.

I'd been in Memphis for four years when I came out of early childhood administration and back into the classroom as an elementary school teacher. I started as a substitute teacher at one of the local elementary/middle schools and had a great experience with the staff and administrators, but something began to change. The more I was in the classroom teaching the children from my perspective as a veteran educator, I realized the curriculum had changed drastically. In many subject areas the curriculum was extensively reformed against the student, in that, the educator is now required to teach the student to the test and not from a foundational perspective that helps them build their skills from one level to the next. On top of that, educators were now being evaluated on the overall student's test performance which is causing many passionate, veteran teachers to lose their careers over students who don't care about their own school performance.

After my second year back in the classroom, teaching middle school students for the first time in my entire career, my husband and I agreed that it was time for me to bow out of the teaching position.

We'd began growing our family together and the stress of my career, being a mother of an infant and trying to be a good wife and mend our marriage, was taking its toll on me. My husband and I wrestled with the decision of me ending my career in education. We knew financially, it was helpful, it sustained us, but in other areas, my career was killing us softly. After much debate, we came to the conclusion that I'd apply for a lesser role in education that didn't require such a demand on my time and my mind.

Applying for jobs with the local school district was coming down to the wire. It was three weeks before school started and the job availabilities were slim to none. I knew I wanted to apply for an assistant teacher position, or assistant anything at this point, but my chances of getting hired this late in the summer were slim. I applied to three open positions; interviewed for two, hired for library assistant.

Say what you want to say, belittle me if you'd like, but when I tell you, God prepared a table specifically for me, I do not tell you a lie. For the last three years of my educational career, God placed me next to the humblest, the most blessed, the most encouraging women and men I've ever worked with in my entire career. What I received from working with that group of individuals was an experience that prepared me for what God was positioning me for next; a season of humility.

From education to hospitality; from a salary to an hourly wage, God had transitioned me from a place of comfort and security, to a place where I was learning to be my husband's help meet, have compassion for others, recognize His voice, and fulfill a specific assignment He had on my life.

My husband and I were in a season of our lives where we needed more income coming in to meet the needs of the family. I'd been out of work for six months and the kids were getting back into the swing of school in the second semester. I could've gone back into the school system and been disobedient to God's instruction, but I wasn't about to take a chance on missing out on what God was about to do in my life.

I had a friend who was working part-time at a restaurant and she shared with me that they were hiring host. I told her I'd apply and I did. After submitting my application on a Thursday evening, I received an email the following Saturday asking if I'd like to schedule an interview the following week. I accepted and text my friend to let her know I'd be interviewing next week and I was looking forward to working with her.

I interviewed with the front of the house manager, whose last question for me was, "And you're applying for a 'host' position, right?"

Before ending the interview, she asked if I'd mind meeting with the general manager before they made a decision to hire me. I accepted and she scheduled the interview.

I go in to meet the general manager and my friend gives me the heads up that they believe I should be applying for a management position instead of a host. She explained to me that the conversation had been going on for two days about the new hire they interviewed.

The general manager finally came to greet me and we moved to the back of the restaurant to begin the interview. He asked the normal interview questions and made small talk. Then he asked the question that turned his lightbulb on, "Why are you applying for a 'host' position at this restaurant.

Once I explained to him that my husband owned a lawn care service and he was in his slow season, I needed to contribute from a financial standpoint, yet still be available for my family, and only needed something part-time his lightbulb came on. His posture shifted and his tone change after I explained. He then shared with me his thoughts about my application and why he needed to meet me before letting me know I was hired. His concern was hiring me for a host position with my extensive professional background. He believed I was selling myself short by taking a host position.

Needless to say, I stepped into my position as a host with humility. I was eager to learn and easy to teach. I wanted to add value to the staff they already had, therefore I was a team player and was flexible when needed. I learned their system fast and was able to demonstrate to them how to be more effective and prcficient so that everyone involved benefited.

It was months after I started hosting that God began to allow ministry to work through me. My position as a host was no longer a job, it was now an assignment. Many of the employees began to open up to me about things they've never shared with anyone. Other's began to be careful with the language they used while in my presence. Prayer was a daily request when I arrived at work and many even explained it as a shift in the atmosphere when I walked into the restaurant. But this one employee was the one that impacted my life the most;

the one who helped me find the beauty in humility.

This young lady had been a host and a trainer for the restaurant for six years at the time. She received her bachelor's degree in political science five years earlier and was planning to leave the restaurant shortly after receiving her degree, but was still there. Upon my employment, the young lady was nothing short of rude to me for many, many, many months. She'd say things about me to others that weren't true. Everything she had to say to me, she said it with an attitude. She'd strategically position me as a greeter/seater and I felt as if she was hoping I'd mess something up and she'd have to correct me; and granted, she did have to correct me a few times, but she was very unprofessional.

She went on a vacation and I had to work her shift for a week. It was then that I learned, every year, she goes on the same vacation to spend time with her brother and nephews in Orlando, FL. That vacation was the very thing that bought her joy. When I learned this I began to pray for her. My prayer for her was that God would begin to put all the pieces of her brokenness back together. I asked God to give her peace and understanding in that season of her life. I wasn't aware of her whole story, but the little I knew compelled me to do something. So I decided that when she came off vacation, I'd attempt to have a conversation with her about her.

After she returned, I saw her renewed. I saw a happy, vibrant, relaxed young lady who was ready to take on the world, then I asked her, "Will you tell me a little about you so we can have a better working relationship?"

She began to share some very intimate information about herself that left me speechless, which is very hard to do. As she continued to share herself with me, I was interceding on her behalf. God began confirming things to me that He'd already shown me in the spirit about her. Then she said, "Stacey, I just feel stuck."

After a few minutes of encouraging her, I asked, "Have you ever done a vision board?"

She was familiar with the concept, but had never completed one, so I shared with her how refreshing and renewing it can be and how looking at it can compel you to do something new, something different. So I told her, I'd bring her everything she needed to complete one and I encouraged her to do it and follow through on the vision that God has shown her He has for her life. I also shared with her that she doesn't have to be stuck anymore and this is where it starts.

The realization is this; you don't begin where you finish. You begin in a place where you may have to crawl before you walk. Look for the assignment within the position; the blessing behind where you're starting, so you may realize that through the test, comes your testimony and your willingness to grow and be strengthened to endure the next assignment God has for you to fulfill.

There was a time in my life when I could be very condescending and very sarcastic, but it was in that season of my life God held my tongue and said, "Wait, be still and the time will come for My grace, My mercy and My glory will show through you," and it did. It was in that season of my life I surrendered to whatever assignment God had for me. I didn't have time to feel like a failure and feel sorry for myself because I was host and not an educator. That was a season in my life that God told me, "Your assignment is to help set my people free, and it will be by your fruit."

I never retaliated on her after the things she did and said to me. I was always loving, always kind and always patient. Had I responded to her in any other way, I would've failed the assignment God had given me.

Never despise small beginnings. You may be the barista at a café and God is setting you up to meet the very people that will help you become one of the world's most inspiring bands. You may be the unit secretary on the ICU and God is setting you up to receive a five-year scholarship for you to complete your nursing education. You may be the kitchen manager at a franchise fast food restaurant and God is setting you up to own the place in ten years. What God has for you is for you. Be encouraged as you walk through your season of making a career choice and not understanding why you're where you are right now. Seek God's plan and purpose for your life. You don't have to continue to feel drained and dismayed in that position you're in. You have the authority to declare God's abundance over your life and find peace right where you are.

    Go ahead! He gave you the authority; use it.

Scriptures that helped me in my surrender:

For who has despised the day of small beginnings? But these seven will be glad when they see the plumb line in the hand of Zerubbabel-these are the eyes of the Lord which range to and fro throughout the earth.
Zechariah 4:10

His master said to him, "Well done, good and faithful slave. You were faithful with a few things, I will put you in charge of many things; enter into the joy of your master."
Matthew 25:23

OH, THAT'S BENEATH ME

SURRENDER YOUR LEADERSHIP

Leadership is not about you. It's about the influence you have on others to make them just as good, if not better, than you. This rang true for my husband when, at the age of twenty-four, he met the recently divorced single mother of two kids, grad student, at The University of Southern Miss.

My husband's a born leader. He was raised in a strict home, very disciplined, loving and he truly valued his family name because he knew, with the name, came a lot of respect. Growing up in a home that required him to man up at an early age, he became very rigid and offensive; and joining the military at the tender age of seventeen, in my opinion, made his rigidity more intense and intolerable.

Naturally loving, he loved hard in intimate relationships when he found a woman worthy enough to share his vulnerability with. But when it came to being a loving, nurturing leader in the home, with his children, his leadership ability as a father suffered.

Aligning leadership with control was my husband's leadership mentality. He came into a family structure as the outsider. His mindset was to come in, establish himself as the head of the house and gain control by force and demand. "What I say goes, your thoughts and opinions don't matter." They felt like soldiers marching to his beat and he was the drill sergeant.

Harsh right? How does the saying go, "You do what you know until you know better?"

Being under an offensive, authoritative, and democratized leadership structure in his home as a child and as a young adult in the military, set the tone for the leadership structure my husband would attempt to bring our house under. Rather quickly, he learned that the leadership structure he was trying to establish needed to be reevaluated and redesigned to meet the current needs and the end results that we were desiring for our family. With the leadership structure we were operating under at that time, we were creating a rollercoaster of emotions in our children, resentment for one another, and a cracked foundation that our empire wouldn't be able to stand upon. We weren't building each other up, we were tearing each other down, piece by piece by piece.

When I met my husband, I wasn't in church regularly. I'd go haphazardly, just to say I went. The longer he and I dated, the more I attended, so I wouldn't have to hear his mouth. Though initially prompted by him, I began going on my own and getting to a place where it was mandatory for me and the kids to attend church and get grounded in Kingdom leadership principles instead of the worldly, democratic leadership principles I was raising them under as a single mother. Then we began going as a family. Initially, we were all getting what we needed; praising, worshipping, relevant and truthful teaching and a loving family atmosphere. We were united, on one accord and my husband had begun leading the house from a place of love, respecting everyone at their level and we were beginning to honor him as the leader of the family. We began looking at him as a leader from a different perspective. His guidance was now constructive, and not judgmental; we were more receptive because he was building us up and stretching us to new levels. But after a while, we stopped growing. It felt like we'd plateaued. We'd reached our lid. What we'd learned had quickly dissipated. We were no longer utilizing the skills, the honor we were once exhibiting had become none existing. We were back to the basics.

You don't know honor until you're taught honor and without honor, there's no leadership building. I didn't know how to honor my husband. I was at a total disadvantage because I didn't grow up seeing honor, therefore, my daughter's didn't understand the importance of honoring him because I didn't model honor. That was my mistake. My husband took on the forceful leadership mentality because of the tone I'd set in the home as a single mother. I'd set up barriers and he was trying to knock them down. I was a single mother with two daughters. Everything was mommy, mommy, mommy. There was no acknowledgement of him; the man of the house, the one to make decisions, and I was to blame for that. I never said, "let me talk to your dad about that," I always made a quick decision and never discussed it with him.

It wasn't until we transitioned into a new local ministry that we began to learn how to honor and what honor looked like. Just like operating a home, a ministry operates under honor. Where there's no honor, there's no leadership. Where there's no leadership, there's chaos, distress and discord.

Well, to say the least, we truly learned honor in that ministry. We attended discipleship classes, leadership development workshops, grief counseling, family and marriage counseling and effective communication courses to help us better understand Kingdom leadership and honor and how the two work together to build a strong foundation of structure, not just in the Kingdom of God, but in our home as well. Through the many tools we took advantage of, we learned what it was to have compassion for people and to meet them where they are in their brokenness. It was truly an eye-opener for my husband and I as we worked at establishing the order of our home and loving each member where they were and for who they were.

My husband and I were quickly placed in leadership roles in the new ministry and honor began to take on a whole new meaning for us. Surrendering our leadership to our spiritual father, our pastor, most said was beneath us, we were now at disadvantage because we were at his mercy. They couldn't have been more wrong. Surrendering our leadership meant, for us, an opportunity to grow; as individuals, as parents, as a spouse, ministry leader, and most of all to experience a deeper relationship with God that would eventually lead us to the exact place God preordained us to be. . . . . Right here!

Our pastor didn't just develop the leaders in us, he cultivated an interminable greatness within us that would impact our children, neighbors, community, this region and ultimately this nation. Surrendering didn't put us at a disadvantage, it actually placed us at an advantage over those who think they can do it alone. We needed to be refined, made new, in order to carry out the assignment God placed on our lives. We'd been leaders in many areas throughout our life. In our careers, as a parent, companion, mentor; we'd played those leadership roles. However, it wasn't until we were taught from a Kingdom perspective, that leadership is far more than directing someone to do something in a moment, but it's about honoring someone enough to understand that where they are guiding you, even when it becomes uncomfortable, is where you are designed to be for a greater purpose than what lies right in front of you.

Scriptures that helped me in my surrender:

Obey your leaders and submit to them, for they are keeping watch over your souls, as those who will have to give an account. Let them do this with joy and not with groaning, for that would be of no advantage to you.
Hebrews 13:17

Remember your leaders, those who spoke to you of God. Consider the outcome of their way of life, and imitate their faith.
Hebrews 13:7

Let the elders who rule well be considered worthy of double honor, especially those who labor in preaching and teaching.
1 Timothy 5:17

THE ENVELOPE

SURRENDER YOUR FINANCES

We stood together, envelope in one hand, fingers intertwined with the other. Forehead to forehand, my husband and I began to pray. This prayer wasn't our average every day prayer. This prayer was specific. This prayer was necessary. This prayer had a power and authority attached to it that we've never prayed before. With God's wonder working word attached to it, we needed His attention and we needed it quickly.

    Four months had passed. Time was down to the wire and we felt like we'd completely run out of resources. Borrowing from Peter to pay Paul was completely exhausted. We'd borrowed from Peter so much that he just wanted his money back so he could sustain. We felt like every turn we made we were hitting a brick wall. We wanted to take a seat and go along for the ride, but we knew where the ride would take us if we just sat there; Homeless! We had three little ones depending on us to make something happen. Going along for the ride was not an option.

In the fourth month, a series of events began to happen in our lives that left our faith weary, us doubting God, and our ability as parents questioned.

I received a call from my husband early one afternoon before leaving the school house and gathering all the kids to head home for the evening.

"The lights have been disconnected," he said.

I was unable to respond. He began to explain to me that he'd paid enough (although we had no money in the bank to pull from) to get the lights back on by midnight, but there was no guarantee.

He asked if I would go to someone's house for a little while until he called to let me know the lights were back on. Hours went by. The kids were getting sleepy. No call from him yet.

I let the kids get so tired so they'd fall asleep on the way home and wouldn't have to experience what we were going through that night.

"Are the lights back on," I text and ask my husband.

"No baby. Y'all come home," he responded.

When we walked through the front door, kids tired and falling over their own feet, I saw my husband, holding a flashlight, sitting on the end of the sofa, reading his Bible and weeping.

That was the first night, in all my years of knowing my husband, I'd ever seen failure on his face.

Two days later, after the lights were back on, I received a letter in the mail from the mortgage company. It read, "If we do not receive the total overdue amount listed below by close of business on this specific date, we will begin the foreclosure process on your home."

We were four months and twenty-six day's delinquent on our mortgage. I dreaded showing that letter to my husband.

My husband was still out mowing lawns. I figured, knowing how he works, I had time to prepare dinner and get the kids settled down for the evening before he arrived home. My intention was to create an atmosphere of comfort and peace for him. I just wanted him to come home and be able to relax after a hard day's work before I shared the letter with him.

The atmosphere was sat and I succeeded in creating the comfort I was hoping for. We enjoyed dinner with the kids, put them down for bed and began enjoying one another's company for the evening. Then I say, "This came in the mail today honey."

He reads the letter for two whole minutes, looks down at his lap, then up at me, and said, "Stacey, I'm sorry," and walked upstairs to our bedroom and closed the door.

Another slap in the face. I was working full-time at the school. He was still managing his lawn care business, but we were smack dab in the middle of his slow season. The holidays were creeping up on us and we weren't making enough money to pay all, if any, of our bills. The first thing that came out was always our tithes, without fail. We managed the rest the best we could, but feeding five mouths, one being an infant, and clothing and diapering were draining us completely dry.

The next morning, I reassured my husband I'd do everything I could to find ways to keep our home and not allow our kids to see the struggle we were going through.

From replacing the transmission in my SUV, to busted pipes in the house that caved in our living room ceiling, my husband and I were in a very dark, low place financially.

While in this season, we were both going through a nine-month discipleship class with our Pastor and a few members from our church. We were growing spiritually, at a very fast pace and we had a zeal for all the knowledge and wisdom we were receiving in the class, but I was still an infant in my walk with God and it showed through my wavering faith within my circumstances.

I still remember when I completely snapped out of it in class one night. It was about four weeks until Founder's Day at our church. That particular Monday night class was about intercessory prayer, boldly asking God to reveal to you what He's asking of you, and agreeing that it's yours and it shall be done. One thing we didn't stop doing was giving. We continued to pay our tithes and we gave what we could give when the opportunity to give more or to sow was presented. But this particular time, God wanted to know how much we really trusted Him. In class that night, I went into prayer at the altar wailing out to God, hoping to hear a response, a solution to all our problems. While I was laid out at the altar, I heard nothing but my own cry out for help. After getting up from the altar, fixing my face and returning to my seat, I began to weep again. This time, it was a softer cry. I'd heard something, but I wasn't sure what it was. My husband handed me another tissue and I wiped my tears away. Then I heard it again. This time louder.

"One thousand dollars."

I remember laying my head on the table and weeping all over again. Then I began to hear more. And more. And more.

It was in that moment that God was sharing with me all the times He was speaking to me, yet I wasn't listening. I was asking, yet I didn't want to hear the answer because it didn't align with the plans I had for me or the circumstances I was going through. It was in that moment that he reminded me about the last sacrificial gift I gave and the amount I gave was less than what He'd instructed. On the ride home, I explained to my husband the exchange I'd had with God and shared with him what God was instructing us to do. I remember saying to my husband at that time, "We can't miss it this time."

    I was tired and if this is what God wanted from me, then by golly, it's done. But where in the world were we going to get a thousand dollars from. Two for that matter because that mandate was also for my husband to give a thousand as well. We talked it through. We were still behind on everything. We still had to pay our tithes. We were unable to see the forest for the trees. It's November, the holiday was coming up and I had two more pay periods before Founder's Day.

    I got it! We were going to pay our tithes and nothing else would be spent from my paychecks until it was time to give on Founder's Day. But there was still the possibility that we were going to come up a little short. My husband began to put some things in place to cover the shortage, if there was one.

We stood together, envelope in one hand, fingers intertwined with the other. Forehead to forehand, my husband and I began to pray. We didn't know what God was going to do in our obedience, but we knew that our prayer would avail much.

It was a February afternoon. At this point, we're both in a place of just trusting God, honoring His word, and praying without ceasing. Three months after giving our Founder's Day sacrificial gift and preparing to give a large amount for our First Fruit, as we do at the beginning of every year, I receive another letter in the mail from the mortgage company. Only this time, the results were in our favor.

Back in November of the year prior, I'd found out about the loan preservation refinancing program we could apply for through the mortgage servicer. Also, there was a government assistance program that would forgive a certain amount of the home mortgage debt if we qualified. This was a very long process and while going through the application process, we weren't allowed to pay anything on our mortgage if we couldn't pay the overdue amount in full. However, one of the stipulations to the application process was that, if we didn't qualify for the home loan preservation program, we would only have sixty days to pay the overdue amount, which had accumulated to over six months, at that point.

My God is FAITHFUL!

Not only did our mortgage get decreased by seventy-five percent, but over thirty-six-thousand dollars of our total loan amount was forgiven.

With everything stacked against us, it took a move of obedience to get us in right standing with God. We had to yield. In surrendering our finances to God we relinquished total control over to Him. He knew how to manage our finances better than we did. So we let him. We are now in a season of our lives where we are sowing where we want to go. It's harvest time and we are reaping from seeds that were sown as far back as fifteen years ago. We have a trust in God that can never be doubted and a faith in Him that never grows weary.

Surrender, you can't afford not to.

Scriptures that helped me in my surrender:

God is not a man that He should lie, nor a son of man that He should repent; Has He said, and will not do it? Or has He spoken, and will He not fulfill it?
Numbers 23:19

Give, and it will be given to you. They will pour into your lap a good measure, pressed down, shaken together, and running over. For by your standard of measure it will be measured to you in return.
Luke 6:38

The Lord will open for you His good storehouse, the heavens, to give rain to your land in its season and to bless all the work of your hands; and you shall lend to many nations, but you shall not borrow. The Lord will make you the head and not the tail, and you only will be above and you will not be underneath, if you listen to the commandments of the Lord, your God, which I charge you today, to observe them carefully,

Deuteronomy 28:12-13

NOT THE ONE

SURRENDER YOUR PERSONAL RELATIONSHIPS

Do you remember that friend or two from grade school that you've always had that close relationship with? You all shared everything; middle school crushes, clothes, your first car, you roomed together on every trip you attended, you even shared your parents with each other. One day, that relationship was no longer what it had been for the past 25 years. You've grown beyond the small talk of what everyone else was doing, you've both started your own family, your kids still call each other aunt/uncle, yet you live in different cities and you've began seeing things from different perspectives. From time to time you all talk about what's going on in your lives but the conversation hasn't been the same since you've started serving in ministry and giving most of your time to the church. You feel the relationship drifting. You know why, but you choose to allow the relationship to take the course it needs to take so there are no hard feelings left behind. You both still love each other, but you're going in two totally different directions.

Time for the shifting.

Many relationships go through the shifting I described above. That relationship shift can be between siblings, friends of the opposite sex, same sex, even a relationship between a parent and child or a family member. Change is inevitable. The most important part of change is how you respond to it.

When many relationships go through a breakup or separation, it can be difficult on one of the individuals involved if not both. Sometimes there's no clarity as to what happened to warrant the separation and then there're some individuals who are left with so many questions unanswered, they just draw their own conclusion, moving on with their life and building resentment for a relationship they concluded to be unfair.

For one reason or another, many people are left feeling rejected in a relationship because there is a lack of communication.

No one communicates when the gap begins to widen. No one talks about how they or maybe things are changing and there needs to be a reevaluation about where the relationship is going or is "this" where it ends.

There are also times when maturity plays a major part in the life of an individual and they begin to outgrow the immaturity of the relationship. That's another shifting. There is a slight and sometimes a considerable change in tendency in one individual, but the other is still not experiencing a renewing of the mind. In the relationship noted above, the shift happened when one individual did not conform to the world, but was transformed by the renewing of the mind. One individual made the choice to transform their mindset to benefit where they wanted to go in life whereas the other wanted to live in the moment they were living, in turn causing the two individuals to begin going in two different directions, cause a gap in their bond, which changed their conversation and ultimately changed the way they began to see one another.

Just like a marriage, a man and a woman come together with different thought processes. They were both raised in different cities, maybe the same city, but different family styles, different social classes, different discipline, different career goals, different expectations placed on them as a child, adolescent, teenager, young adult and now man and woman. They are bringing all those differences together to form one family with the same goal in mind. Do you realize how difficult that is? How do you bring all those differences together to make a harmonious environment for everyone involved?

You surrender.

The harmony begins when you surrender.

Have you ever thought to pray about a relationship you are contemplating getting involved in? Have you ever thought to ask God to place people in your life for the purpose of impact, growth, discipline, or guidance?

Why not?

The Bible tells us to not be deceived: "Bad company ruins good morals" (1

Corinthians 15:33). Simply put, be careful of the company you keep.

It is critical that in the personal relationships you seek, ask God what is its' purpose. Not everyone you meet will have your best interest at heart. Not everyone you meet will be able to speak into your life. By their fruit, you will recognize them (Matthew 7:16). You also have to be grounded in the word of God, discerning who to let in and who to walk away from. Remember, someone else is also asking God to place people in their life that has His heart. Someone is out there looking for you, just waiting for you to show them your fruit.

Every morning I wake up, during my time with God, I ask Him to place me in the life of someone whom I can impact. I ask Him for the words to say and the actions to take in dealing with the people I interact with on a daily basis. I also ask Him if it's my day to just be impacted by an encouraging word that He has sent someone to give me. Give me the discernment to know the difference Lord. Trust God in choosing your relationships for you. If He tells you that's 'not the one,' believe Him.

That's how I choose to develop my personal relationships today. I have to watch who I let into my circle. My spirit is too important for me to jeopardize for a feeling of emotional pleasure that will only last a moment. I need people in my life who are going to push me to a place where I wouldn't push myself; to a place that may be uncomfortable but it's taking me exactly where I need to be. . . . . . closer to God. I need people in my life that I can continue to strengthen and grow with spiritually. A person who hasn't been where I'm going can't lead me to a place they've never been. If I chose to allow that type of person to guide me, I'm not going very far. I can't afford to waste time on or with people who only want to sit around and talk about what someone else is or isn't doing, and neither can you. Too many people are hurting and God has an assignment for you to do.

Over the past ten years, God's been placing people in my life and me in theirs on purpose. It may have been only for a season. Maybe for them to show me something or for me to show them something, but whichever impact it was, I've had the opportunity to meet some very beautiful people. I thank God for that opportunity. Each and every one of them have given me a joy, even in the separation of some of those relationships, that I wouldn't have experienced had it not been for the divine assignment that connected us.

My current relationships have balance. We don't agree on everything, but our interactions are filled with the love of Christ and the truth in knowing where we are as individuals, in our spiritual life and our emotional health.

Scriptures that helped me in my surrender:

A man of many companions may come to ruin, but there is a friend who sticks closer than a brother.
Proverb 18:24

Greater love has no one than this, that someone lay down his life for his friend.
John 15:13

Iron sharpens iron, and one man sharpens another.
Proverb 27:17

Acknowledgements

None of this would be possible without God's amazing grace. I can't be more grateful enough that He chose me! Lost, broken and confused, I was like a leaf in the wind, blowing from here to there, but God captured me. He placed me in a season of preservation until I was well enough to start serving His Kingdom.

"Thank you God for your amazing grace and your renewing mercy."

To my biggest fan, the most influential person in my life, my husband; you have been more to me than you can imagine. Your encouraging words, the constructive criticism, even when I didn't want to hear it, made me feel like I could conquer the world. You pushed me to places I was denying myself, yet you knew, I was readily prepared to walk out the assignment at that time in my life. You saved me! You made sure I was in right standing with God; and although that was the toughest season of our life together, you obeyed God's instructions and prompted me, through your actions, to surrender my life to God. I can never repay you for that.

To my loving children; thank you for the sacrifice. For the past year, you all have given up movie night, weekend outings and date nights to allow me to complete this book. I can't make up that time, but know this, you've been a part of something much bigger than us. Something that, for the rest your lives, will directly impact the people around you; many you will meet, many you won't.

Megan, thank you for stretching me as a mother and for showing me my true potential. Morgan, thank you for loving me and being so flexible. Landen, thank you for the prayers and encouragement that helped me make it through many cloudy days. And Maddox, just thank you; your kisses have given me life.

To my Pastor and First Lady; thank you for knowing my heart. Thank you for modeling honor, respect, love, and leadership to me at a time in my life when I needed it the most. You all are one of the reasons this book is what it is, not just for me, but for my readers as well; a blessing!

    To my family, friends, co-workers, and clients, you have inspired me to be more; more compassionate, transparent, reliable, loving, intentional and supportive. Every day, you give me hope, that today is first day of the best days of your life. Thank you for the encouragement, excitement, and the laughter. I couldn't have done this without you.

Made in United States
Troutdale, OR
06/27/2024